Christopher Columbus

Pocket BIOGRAPHIES

Series Editor C.S. Nicholls

Highly readable brief lives of those who have played a significant part in history, and whose contributions still influence contemporary culture.

Pocket **BIOGRAPHIES**

Christopher Columbus

PETER RIVIÈRE

SUTTON PUBLISHING

First published in the United Kingdom in 1998 by
Sutton Publishing Limited · Phoenix Mill
Thrupp · Stroud · Gloucestershire · GL5 2BU

British Library Cataloguing in Publication Data
A catalogue record for this book is available from the British
Library.

ISBN 0-7509-1876-4

 ALAN SUTTON™ and SUTTON™ are the
trade marks of Sutton Publishing Limited

Typeset in 13/18 pt Perpetua.
Typesetting and origination by
Sutton Publishing Limited.
Printed in Great Britain by
The Guernsey Press Company Limited
Guernsey, Channel Islands.

C O N T E N T S

ACKNOWLEDGEMENTS

I am very grateful to Alison Brown who undertook the picture research for this volume and to Alina Darbellay who pursued in the Strahov Library of the Royal Canonry of the Premonstratensians, Prague, what unfortunately turned out to be a red herring.

I also wish to acknowledge my thanks for permission to quote passages from Christopher Columbus, *Journal of the First Voyage* (Aris & Phillips Ltd, 1990), Felipe Fernández-Armesto, *Columbus* (Oxford University Press, 1991), J.M. Cohen, *The Four Voyages of Christopher Columbus* (Penguin Books, 1988), Fernando Colón, *The Life of the Admiral Christopher Columbus* (Rutgers University Press, 1960). Certain passages have also been cited from Samuel Morison, *Journals and Other Documents on the Life and Voyages of Christopher Columbus* (1963), but attempts to find the present copyright holder of this work have so far proved unsuccessful. I am no less grateful and should this information be forthcoming the omission will be corrected in any future edition.

CHRONOLOGY

c. 1451	Columbus born in Genoa
1472	Columbus working in family weaving business
c. 1476	Columbus moves to Lisbon
c. 1479	Columbus marries Felipa Perestrello e Moniz
1480	Columbus's elder son, Diego, born
1485–6	Columbus seeks help for his enterprise from the monarchs of Aragon and Castile – Ferdinand and Isabella
1488	**November.** Columbus's second son, Fernando, born to Beatriz Enríquez
1492	**January.** Columbus receives royal permission for project
	3 August. Sails from Palos, Spain
	12 August. Arrives at the Canary Islands
	6 September. Leaves the Canaries heading westward
	12 October. Makes landfall in the Bahamas
	28 October. Discovers Cuba
	6 December. Reaches Hispaniola
	24 December. Columbus's flagship, the *Santa María*, wrecked
	25 December. Puerto Navidad founded on Hispaniola

Chronology

1493	**16 January.** Columbus sets out for home

1493
16 January. Columbus sets out for home
15 March. Arrives back at Palos
25 September. Columbus departs on his second Atlantic crossing
3 November. Arrives off island of Dominica
18 November. Discovers Puerto Rico
28 November. Finds garrison of Puerto Navidad massacred

1494 **April–September.** Explores Cuba and Jamaica

1495 **March.** Starts year-long campaign to subdue interior of Hispaniola

1496 **10 March.** Columbus departs for Spain
11 June. Arrives Cádiz

1498 **30 May.** Columbus departs on his third Atlantic crossing via the Cape Verde Islands
31 July. Columbus arrives off Trinidad and goes on to explore coast of mainland South America
19 August. Arrives on Hispaniola to find revolt underway

1498–1500 Columbus suppresses uprising on Hispaniola

1500 **September–October.** Columbus arrested and returned to Spain

1502 **3 April.** Columbus departs on fourth Atlantic crossing
15 June. Reaches Martinique
29 June. Arrives at Hispaniola but in accordance with royal command is not allowed to land

1503	**July–May.** Explores Caribbean coast of Central America
	June. Marooned on Jamaica
1504	**June.** Columbus and men rescued and taken to Hispaniola
	12 September. Columbus departs for Spain
	7 November. Arrives back in Spain
1505	**Summer.** Columbus in ill health
1506	**20 May.** Columbus dies in Valladolid

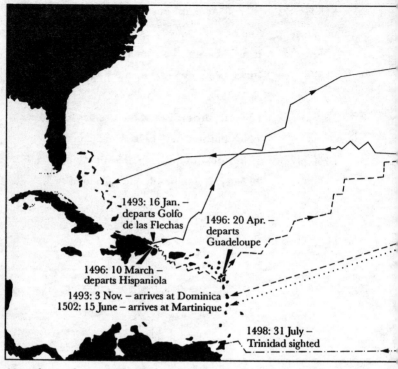

Map indicating the course of Columbus's four crossings of the Atlantic Ocean.

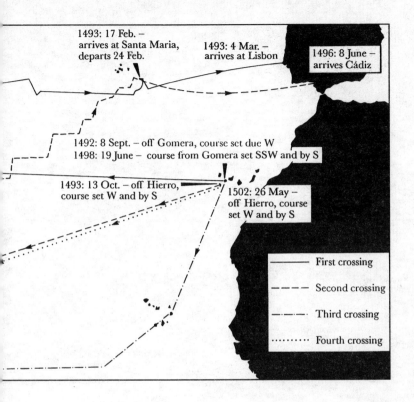

1493: 17 Feb. – arrives at Santa Maria, departs 24 Feb.

1493: 4 Mar. – arrives at Lisbon

1496: 8 June – arrives Cádiz

1492: 8 Sept. – off Gomera, course set due W
1498: 19 June – course from Gomera set SSW and by S

1493: 13 Oct. – off Hierro, course set W and by S

1502: 26 May – off Hierro, course set W and by S

———————	First crossing
– – – – –	Second crossing
–·–·–·–	Third crossing
············	Fourth crossing

INTRODUCTION

The repercussions of Christopher Columbus's landfall in the Bahamas on 12 October 1492 have still not died away as the events surrounding its five hundredth anniversary in 1992 bear witness. These ranged from the construction of the hugely expensive Faro a Colón (Columbus lighthouse) at Santo Domingo in the Dominican Republic to innumerable conferences and publications. By no means was everything celebratory, because for many Christopher Columbus was not a hero who found a New World, but a villain responsible for exposing that world to the destruction of its civilizations and the death of millions of its inhabitants.

A man of obscure background, his feat in being the first to sail across the Atlantic has made him a household name in the western world. There are, of course, his detractors who deny Columbus his achievement and instead argue that the honour of finding the Americas belongs in the first instance to the ancestors of the present native peoples, and, if to a European then St Brendan, the Vikings or someone else deserves the credit. While it may be the case that Europeans had made their way to the Americas before Columbus, it is equally the case that their efforts did not have lasting historical consequences. Finally, there is even a school of thought that dismisses the very idea of Europeans discovering anything on the basis that you cannot find what no one has lost, least of all the people there already.

Like America, if not actually lost, Columbus's historic voyage remained relatively unheralded until the nineteenth century when Columbus was adopted as a national hero by the rapidly growing United States of America, which was in search of an identity. The popularity of Columbus was in part due to Washington Irving's *The Life and Voyages of Christopher Columbus*, published in 1828 and of which some 175 editions appeared before 1900. It was triumphalist in its approach and the source of many of the myths that surround Columbus. It was not until the years leading up to the four hundredth anniversary of his crossing in 1892 that serious historical assessment, using most of the sources available today, resulted in a more balanced approach. However, even if today his fame is so widespread that Christopher Columbus must rank among the most famous historical names in the world, few people could tell you more about him than that he found America. While, of course, this achievement must be central to any account of his life, the reader will also learn in these pages about his later and less famous voyages of discovery, of a journey through life that see-sawed through triumph and disaster, the latter often appearing to be of his own making. It will be argued in the final chapter that Columbus was a difficult man, but that it is unlikely that anyone who was not of such a temperament would have achieved what he did. It required a degree of obstinacy, determination and self-centredness that inevitably makes the lives of the individual and of those around him uncomfortable.

It is necessary to say a few words about some of the early sources on which this and other biographies are inevitably based. Because of his humble origins, little is known about his early years and Columbus himself remained silent on the subject in his writings. Indeed so little is known that even his country of origin has been a matter of dispute with different people making claims for

Spanish, French, Corsican and Portuguese descent, as well as many other nationalities. Even if his later life is better documented, there is still a great deal of speculation and there are numerous conflicting views about his actions and motivations. Indeed, some writers seem intent on making Columbus more mysterious than he is and have, for example, argued that his achievement could only have been possible if he were a spy in the service of the Portuguese crown. In a work of this length and nature it is not possible nor appropriate to take into account, let alone try to resolve, any of the numerous arguments that rage around Columbus and what he did. Rather, the aim must be to tell the life of Columbus as far as it is known and agreed.

The obvious and most important sources regarding Christopher Columbus are his own writings. Unfortunately, although he wrote extensively about his voyages and discoveries, very little of the original remains and what we have is a version copied and edited by the sixteenth-century human rights activist Bartolomé de Las Casas. Much of the material is contained in his *History of the Indies*, a work completed in 1552, and there is also his version of Columbus's own logbook of the first crossing, *The First Voyage*. Unfortunately Las Casas paraphrased much of the latter, putting it into the third person rather than citing verbatim and making his own additions, so that it is not always easy to know what is Columbus, what has been left out and what has been put in. In some instances it is obvious. For example, a reference to Florida must be Las Casas's addition since it was not discovered until seven years after Columbus died. Even allowing for these drawbacks, Columbus's logbook as presented to us by Las Casas has been extensively quoted in order to achieve a sense of immediacy in the story. Another invaluable source is the biography of Columbus written by his younger son, Fernando Colón. This was first published in 1571 in Italian but it should be remembered that not only was a son writing about his father but perhaps also that the work was prepared for a purpose, as part of the defence of Columbus's activities from the attempts by the Spanish monarchs to strip his heirs of the privileges and titles bestowed on the family.

These are the main contemporary sources, together with some lesser ones, that have been employed in the preparation of this biography. No attempt has been made to translate these sources into English for the purposes of this volume. Rather, existing English translations have been used, mostly published quite recently and thus relatively accessible to anyone who, on reading this introductory biography, wishes to delve further into Columbus's life. For example, for Columbus's journal of his first crossing I have relied on Ife's 1990 translation, published in paperback. As well as the early documents there are numerous secondary sources and many full-length biographies of Columbus; the titles of some of these, once again mainly recently published works, are to be found in the bibliography.

There are no contemporary portraits of Columbus and the pictures we have of him portray him with varied looks and an array of costumes. On the other hand, the few descriptions of him written by those who knew him are remarkably consistent. The following is that left to us by his younger son, Fernando:

> The Admiral was a well-built man of more than average stature, the face long, the cheeks somewhat high, his body neither fat nor lean. He had an aquiline nose and light-coloured eyes; his complexion too was light and tending to bright red. In youth his hair was

blond, but when he reached the age of thirty, it turned all white. In eating and drinking, and in the adornment of his person, he was very moderate and modest. He was affable in conversation with strangers and very pleasant to the members of his household, though with a certain gravity. He was so strict in the matters of religion that for fasting and saying prayers he might have been taken for a member of a religious order.[1]

THE EARLY YEARS

C hristopher Columbus was born in Genoa in about 1451. His father, Domenico, was a weaver, and his mother, Susanna Fontanarossa, also came from a weaving family. We know of a sister, Bianchinetta, and two younger brothers, Bartolomé and Diego, who were to be his companions and supporters throughout his life. He received little in the way of formal education and the claim that he attended the University of Pavia, where he is meant to have studied geography, astronomy and geometry, is almost certainly not true. If later in life he was recognized for his knowledge of these subjects it was because he was self-taught. As a young boy he was engaged in his father's business, although at an early age he started going to sea. This was not altogether surprising since, along with Venice, Genoa was the great trading city of the Mediterranean.

As a result of the fall of Constantinople to the Turks in 1453, Genoa's extensive trade networks in the eastern Mediterranean and beyond were severely disrupted and the Genoese trading families turned their attention westward. One of the last of the Genoese trading centres in the eastern Mediterranean was Chios, which Columbus visited in about 1473. If his own record is correct, he was in Tunisia a year earlier on a raiding party to capture an Aragonese ship. According to Columbus, the crew of the boat he was on mutinied and wanted to turn back, but he tricked them by altering the compass so they thought they were sailing towards Marseilles when they were actually heading for Tunis. In 1476, Columbus turned his interest westward and arrived in Lisbon, according to some versions accidentally. He was involved in a Genoese trading expedition to England and Flanders when, off Cape St Vincent, an attack by pirates resulted in the destruction of the convoy and Columbus only saved himself by swimming 6 miles.

From Lisbon he was involved on behalf of Genoese trading companies with voyages as far north as Iceland, which included visits to Bristol and Galway and as far south as the Gulf of Guinea.

Thus before he attempted his Atlantic crossing he had not only first-hand knowledge of the Mediterranean but also of those parts of the Atlantic Ocean which were regularly navigated at that time by Portuguese, Spanish and English ships. He would also have heard sailors' stories of what lay further out in the Atlantic. These may have ranged from information about Greenland and Labrador contained in Icelandic sagas to accounts of strange flotsam washed up in the Canary Islands. There is the story, although probably apocryphal, of the dying helmsman who passed Columbus a map of the ocean. During the fifteenth century there was intense interest in the frontier that the Atlantic, or Ocean Sea as it was known, presented. Exploration had proceeded south down the coast of Africa but no one had ventured far to the west. This lack of knowledge had not prevented cartographers of the time from speculating and filling their maps with such imagined islands as Antillia or Brasil.

In order to understand better what Columbus thought he was doing it is worth taking a brief look at the cosmological ideas in circulation at the time. It was widely accepted in the late fifteenth century that the world was round but this was a theory that had yet to be demonstrated. What was not known was the length of its circumference. Various calculations had been made, but all of them were under-estimations, and some dramatically so. One of the main authorities was Ptolemy, the Alexandrian geographer of the second century AD, who proposed a world of 360 degrees, half land and half water, the ocean part stretching from the most westerly point of Europe to the most easterly of Asia. There was not, however, agreement about the eastward extension of the Asian continent and accordingly the width of the ocean. Furthermore, there was a school of thought that advocated an antipodean landmass in the middle of the ocean which balanced that of the known world. These geographical ideas are important in trying to understand what Columbus had intended to do.

What was Columbus's objective in sailing westward? The common and popular answer to this question is that he was trying to reach Cathay and the Indies by this route, but there were other possible aims. One, rather less ambitious, was to discover the islands, similar to the Canaries, Azores and Cape Verde, that were assumed to exist out in the Atlantic Ocean. A third possibility was to discover the Antipodes. These aims are by no means exclusive, and having more than one arrow to one's bow when one cannot be certain what the target is, is not a bad idea. Indeed when Columbus returned, although he insisted that he had reached the Orient, others thought he had merely found more islands or the Antipodes. What is quite clear is that Columbus did not just sail off into the blue; his voyage was the next step in the exploration of the ocean frontier and in line with accepted geographical knowledge. It was a matter of who was to take that step.

Experience of maritime navigation, however, was not in itself enough to mount an expedition of the sort that Columbus was to propose. Patronage was also required. Columbus achieved this in three ways: through his Genoese connections, his marriage and royal favour. The Genoese mercantile network was made up of rich families who had settled in important trading centres and often achieved considerable influence there. Columbus became associated with the powerful Centurione family and others in Lisbon, for whom he undertook commercial voyages in the Atlantic. We can assume that it was through these contacts that he was able to marry, in about 1479, Felipa

Perestrello e Moniz, the daughter of a lesser noble family, but still noble enough to give the weaver's son a degree of social respectability and status which he had previously lacked. Her father had been associated with the Portuguese king, Henry the Navigator, and as a reward for the part he played in capturing the Madeira Islands had received the governorship of the small and barren island of Porto Santo where Columbus may have spent as long as two years. Felipa bore him a son and heir, Diego, in 1480, but died soon after.

Whereas powerful friends and financial support were necessary attributes to undertake explorations, they were not sufficient. To be successful royal patronage was needed, for whatever land a private individual might discover, he could not lay claim to it, or sovereignty over it, without the backing of royalty. Furthermore, if, as is likely in the case of Columbus, he was not looking just for wealth, but also status and honours, royal recognition was even more important. Columbus's first attempt at securing royal support was probably made to King João II of Portugal, perhaps in 1484. It was an obvious and sensible choice. Not only was Columbus in Lisbon where he had connections, but João II was committed to the continued Portuguese exploration of the Atlantic coast of Africa. However, if Columbus followed the obvious course and solicited the Portuguese king's patronage he failed to obtain it. The reason seems to have been the rejection of his geographical calculations. To understand this we must return to contemporary cosmography.

If Ptolemy's reckoning of a world of half land and half ocean was accepted, then such a vast expanse of water made any hope of a successful outcome to Columbus's project out of the question. Accordingly Columbus, by the selective use of other sources, managed to reduce the number of degrees of water between the Canary Islands and Japan by two-thirds, to a mere 60 degrees. For the position of Japan (or Cipangu) he relied on the thirteenth-century writings of Marco Polo, who had placed this island some 1,500 miles east of China. This distance, however, still represented a voyage of prodigious endurance, but Columbus managed a further calculation in his favour. The accepted length of a degree at the equator was 60 nautical miles, but Columbus, by misinterpreting the tenth-century Arabian cosmographer al-Farghani, reduced this so that the circumference of his world was an underestimation by some 25 per cent. While the result of these calculations made the journey now seem a feasible proposition, the panel of experts set up by King João to consider the matter declined to accept them. One of Columbus's mistakes may have been to rely too heavily on Marco Polo, for whereas there were those who accepted his veracity, there were many who were far more sceptical. Tradition has it that Columbus was rejected either because of his reliance on Marco Polo and on his extreme easterly positioning of Japan, or because of the excessive demands for reward he made in the event of success, or as his son put it:

> . . . being a man of noble and lofty ambitions, would not covenant save on such terms as would bring him great honour and advantage, in order that he might leave a title and estate befitting the grandeur of his works and merits.[1]

Following this setback, Columbus looked elsewhere for support. At that time there was no kingdom of Spain; rather the Iberian Peninsula was divided into four Christian kingdoms: Castile, Aragon, Navarra and Portugal (and until 1492 the Moorish kingdom of Granada, which became incorporated into

Castile). The kingdoms of Aragon and Castile, which for ease of reference will jointly be referred to as Spain, had been joined by the marriage of their respective monarchs, Ferdinand and Isabella, and it was to them that Columbus transferred his search for patronage.

Columbus's move was not a step into the dark as relations of his dead wife lived in Huelva just across the border from Portugal. There he entered into a relationship with a Spanish woman, Beatriz Enríquez de Arana, by whom he had his son, Fernando, in November 1488. There has been much argument about the status of Beatriz; one side claiming that she was little more than a servant and the other that she came from a well-to-do family of wine producers. Whichever is the truth, the fact is that Columbus never regularized their union and their relationship seems to have been fairly short-lived. Even so, Columbus obviously felt some responsibility for her and bestowed upon her the reward that he claimed for being the first to sight land on his epic crossing. Furthermore, in 1505, not long before his death, Columbus directed his legitimate son, Diego, to treat her like his own mother and to see that she received financial support.

Although Columbus appreciated that he would require royal support, he began his search at a more humble level and approached two noblemen who had been active in Spanish expansion in the Canary Islands, the Count of Medinaceli and the Duke of Medina Sidonia. Through their good offices he obtained an audience with Isabella in Córdoba during January 1486. Columbus seems to have impressed the queen, especially perhaps with his vision that the gold he brought back from the Orient should be used to free Jerusalem from the infidels. Certainly the monarchs were interested enough in what he proposed to keep him at their expense through most of 1486 and 1487 while the matter was looked into more closely. In the summer of 1486 a commission under the chairmanship of Hernando de Talavera, Isabella's confessor and later Archbishop of Granada, was set up. It initially met in Córdoba but later moved with the court to Salamanca, the scene of one of the popular stories surrounding Columbus. This version represents Columbus as the practical down-to-earth navigator who overcame the theoretical and dogmatic flat-earth arguments put forward by the professors of the university. In fact, the matter in question was not whether the earth was flat but, as previously, the size of the globe. The members of the commission, who were not entirely dismissive of the project, were rightly sceptical about Columbus's calculations and did not recommend support for it.

Ferdinand and Isabella neither rejected nor accepted the commission's report but the project seemed doomed to remain in limbo, especially following the rounding of the Cape of Good Hope by the Portuguese explorer Bartolomeu Diaz in 1488, which appeared to open an eastward sea route to the Orient. Columbus, however, did not take rejection lightly and immediately started looking elsewhere. In 1488 he renewed contact with the Portuguese king who invited him to return, which he did briefly although nothing came of it. In the following year Columbus sent his brother Bartolomé to seek the help of either Charles VIII of France or Henry VII of England, but without success. At the same time he continued his efforts in Spain. Columbus himself had very little economic or political clout but despite this he put together a rich and influential band of supporters, both at court and elsewhere. It is not clear how he managed this, but in the end it can probably be put down to his own personal qualities, his powers of persuasion, deep-seated convictions and a driving ambition.

Two of Columbus's most powerful allies were Luis de Santángel (also Keeper of the Privy Purse to the King) and Francesco Pinelli, and it was probably these two men who engineered his summons to court, then at Santa Fé near Granada, at the end of 1491. This was a historic moment for on 2 January 1492, Granada, the last Moorish stronghold in Spain, surrendered and a preoccupation of the past centuries, the removal of the Moors from Spain, disappeared. It is doubtful whether Columbus joined in any celebrations for the same month another panel of experts rejected his proposal yet again. He had left to return to Seville when there occurred one of those amazing reversals of fortune. He had not gone far before he was called back to be told that he could, after all, make his voyage. What caused this sudden change of heart is not certain, but the likelihood is that some sort of financial package had finally been assembled; often it is the case that the words of experts and scientists are ignored if other influences, such as power and money, intervene. Tradition has it that it was

Santángel who brokered a deal; the largest contribution was provided by Santángel and Pinelli, who secured their loan against the sale of indulgences, while the rest was made up by commercial interests. This was the famous occasion on which Isabella reputedly pawned her jewels in order to support Columbus, but there seems to be little truth in the story. On the other hand, royal support for the venture was clearly vital and Santángel may well have been responsible for persuading Isabella that she had little to lose and much to gain by backing the project, and much to lose by not.

Given the fact that acceptance of his proposal was clearly a borderline decision, Columbus's demands for his undertaking seem excessive. Even so, he got what he wanted although it must be remembered that it was on a 'no win, no fee' basis, so that the sovereigns were not taking a very great risk. His rewards were laid out in the so-called *Capitulations* of 17 April 1492 and consisted of five clauses. First, he was to be appointed admiral of all the islands and lands he discovered and his title, Admiral of the Ocean Sea, together with all rights and prerogatives were to pass to his heirs in perpetuity. Second, he was to be appointed viceroy and governor-general of all the lands he discovered. Third, he had the right to 10 per cent of the value of all precious stones and metals, spices, merchandise and other products derived from these lands. Fourth, he or his deputy was to have the right to adjudicate any dispute involving such items, and lastly he was to have the option of paying one-eighth of the total expense of any ship sailing to the new lands in return for one-eighth of the profit.

On 30 April the article concerning the titles and the right of Columbus's heirs to them was repeated in the so-called *Title*, although once again the granting of them was dependent on success. At the same time other documents were also provided including a passport to the Indies and a Letter of Credence bearing the greetings of the Spanish sovereigns to whatever potentates, perhaps the Great Khan of China or the Emperor of Japan, whom Columbus might meet. Finally, there was a letter directing the provision of two caravels for Columbus's use. These the sovereigns managed to provide very cheaply as the directive was aimed at the community of Palos near Seville, which owed them as the penalty for a past conviction for smuggling. The original idea had been that the crews would be recruited from among those against whom there were civil or penal proceedings, the proceedings being suspended for the volunteers. Thus arose the story that Columbus's ships were crewed by gaolbirds. In fact experienced crews manned the ships, although whether they would have been forthcoming without the intervention of Martín Alonso Pinzón is another matter. Pinzón was a local man and highly respected as an experienced mariner. He seems to have been one of Columbus's supporters in the lobbying that led up to 1492, for he may well have entertained ambitions similar to Columbus's, although possessed of rather different qualities. He and Columbus were suspicious of each other from the start but their co-operation was born of necessity; they needed one another. Of the ninety men who sailed with Columbus the names of eighty-seven have been identified and all save five, including Columbus himself, were Spanish. Most of them were local men who owed allegiance as much to Pinzón as to Columbus, and it may be wondered whether they would have ventured with Columbus on such a perilous journey into an unknown ocean if Pinzón had not been going too. Among the crew was a converted Jew, who spoke Hebrew, Chaldean and some Arabic and thus, it was thought, would be able to act as an interpreter of oriental languages. There were also two representatives of the sovereigns on board, whose job it was to look after royal interests and whose presence suggests greater expectations on the part of Ferdinand and Isabella than they are often credited with.

T W O

ACROSS THE ATLANTIC

The little fleet of three ships that Columbus commanded is one of the most famous in history, but our knowledge of it is very slight. It included Columbus's flagship, *Santa María*, originally called *Gallega* because it was built in Galicia in north-west Spain and owned by Juan de la Cosa from whom it was chartered. The ship's overall length was about 80 ft, and for the crossing it had a crew of about forty. It was the only ocean-going vessel in the fleet and was not technically a caravel, although in popular tradition it is almost invariably referred to as such. The other two ships, those provided by Palos, were smaller, their overall lengths probably being under 70 ft. They were the *Pinta*, owned by Cristóbal Quintero, commanded by Martín Pinzón with his younger brother Francisco as master, and the *Niña*, owned by Juan Niño, commanded by Vicente Yáñez Pinzón, another brother of Martín. Both these vessels had a crew of about twenty-five.

Columbus led this fleet out of Palos on Friday 3 August 1492. The first leg was the familiar route to the Canary Islands, although it did not pass without some problems. The *Pinta*'s rudder broke and Columbus suspected that this was engineered by the owner Cristóbal Quintero who was reluctant to let his boat go on the expedition. The boat was left floundering off Gran Canaria while Columbus pushed on to Gomera, arriving there on 12 August, to see whether he could find a replacement vessel. There was none available so Columbus returned to oversee repairs to the *Pinta* and the whole fleet finally assembled at Gomera on 2 September. It has been claimed that the expedition hung around while Columbus dallied with Beatríz de Bobadilla, the widow of the Governor of Gomera and now governor in her own right, whom he may well have known in Córdoba some years earlier. If he did, it was not for long. The boats were quickly stocked with supplies and on 6 September the fleet sailed westwards, into the unknown.

It is perhaps difficult to comprehend just what was being undertaken. Very few journeys in the history of the world have taken place literally into the unknown. Most maritime exploration up until then, as for example the contemporary voyages south to the Cape of Good Hope, had not involved long periods out of sight of land, the possible exception being the remarkable Polynesian migrations in the Pacific. Even if in modern times astronauts have travelled where none has gone before, they, their support team and any other observers know exactly where they are going and where they are at all times. None of this was true of Columbus and his crew. They may have thought they knew where they were going but they could not be sure, and once they were out of sight of land neither they nor anyone else knew exactly where they were.

The question that has often been raised of why Columbus dipped as far south as the Canaries to start his crossing has two answers. First, the most easterly point of Asia, the island of Cipangu (Japan) was thought to be on the same latitude as the Canary Islands, the most westerly land under Spanish control. Second, the presence at this latitude of the north-east trade winds that blew steadily to the west was generally known among mariners who frequented the African coast. If the former belief was not correct (and given that no European had visited Japan this inaccuracy is hardly surprising), the latter was almost exactly right, which meant that in his first attempt Columbus almost took the best route to the Americas and in his second, setting course slightly further south, did just that, travelling a route that was to be followed throughout the age of sail. Indeed, so firmly set were the winds carrying the fleet westward that concern arose among the crew as to whether it would be possible to find a wind to take them back home. On 22 September, during a period of variable winds, Columbus noted: 'I was in great need of this head-wind because my men were very agitated and thought that no winds blew on these seas that would get them back to Spain'.[1] However, this refers specifically to the concerns of the crew and not Columbus and it seems unlikely that if he was aware of the existence of the trade winds, he would have been ignorant of the westerlies that blew at more northerly latitudes. Indeed, on the return journey Columbus set a more northerly route with the obvious intention of picking up those winds.

This problem of distance from home and how to return there seems to have been something that he had anticipated from the outset. On 9 September, the day that the last sight of land, the island of Hierro, slipped below the horizon, he wrote in the log. 'He made 15 leagues that day and decided to reckon fewer than he was making so that if the journey were long the men should not feel afraid and discouraged'.[2] Adjustments of distance of this order continued throughout the voyage so that by 1 October, for example, the total distance covered was 707 leagues but the public record showed only 584. Some people have accepted Columbus at his word, believing that the falsification was designed to prevent anxiety among the crew. Others have pointed out that there were among the crew navigators at least, if not those more experienced than Columbus who would be keeping their own records. Even so, discrepancy between navigators was almost inevitable as marine navigation at that time was still in its infancy and few instruments existed to help sailors when on the open ocean.

The instruments available were the compass, hourglass, which had to be turned every half-hour and was thus prone to error, a crude log for measuring speed and, for astronomical observations, the quadrant and the astrolabe. The latter is a more complex version of the former, but both are almost impossible to use with any accuracy on the swaying deck of a ship. Navigators also relied on their experiential knowledge and observation; for example, speed could be gauged by the length of time a wave took to pass from the bow to stern.

Using these instruments and methods, and even the naked eye as long as the pole star was visible, an experienced navigator could judge with a fair degree of accuracy his latitude, but there was still no way, nor would there be for nearly another 300 years, of accurately fixing longitude. So, whereas Columbus, who was a master seaman and navigator, was able to maintain a steady westerly course, he had no secure means of measuring how far he had travelled westward, or, of course, how far he had to travel. The expedition also ran into another unexpected navigational problem, not previously encountered and which gave rise to some concern. Although easterly magnetic variation, that is the position of magnetic north to the east of true north, was known about, the journey across the Atlantic brought the fleet into the zone of westerly variation for the first time. Columbus duly observed this, although he was not at first certain how to account for it because the current belief was that the pole star was fixed at true north. However, his explanation that the compass held steady but the pole star moved turned out to be accurate because, in fact, the star is not fixed but describes a radius round true north.

Columbus also carried with him a map, although given that he was sailing into uncharted territory it is difficult to know of what use he thought it might be. Even so, we know that he and Martín Pinzón used it at a crucial stage in the voyage to justify their location and actions. On 25 September, the two men agreed to the accuracy of the chart with reference to the islands marked on it, but reckoned that the fleet had been pushed to the north-east by currents and it had not yet sailed far enough to find them. This can only have been a ruse to keep the crew happy, for from early in the voyage every sign that could possibly be taken to indicate the proximity of land was so taken. Thus on 14 September there was the sighting of a tern and a tropic bird which, it was claimed, never go more than 25 leagues from land. On 18 September it was a bank of clouds on the horizon that was evidence and the following day a rainstorm without wind, something which, it was said, does not occur at sea. Three days later, the presence of whales was interpreted in the same manner. There were also inevitably false sightings of land, such as that by Pinzón on 26 September, which raised the hopes of the crew only for them to be dashed again. By early October, the situation had worsened considerably; morale was low, mutiny was in the air. Las Casas tells us that part of the crew, convinced that they were heading for certain death for the sake of the mad ambitions of a foreigner, plotted to throw Columbus overboard, agreeing to say that he had fallen into the sea while trying to take sightings with his astrolabe. There was also tension between Columbus and Pinzón, the latter wanting to steer south-west to Japan and the former to keep due west for the mainland of the Indies. On 7 October, the fleet altered course to the south-west to follow a flock of birds but by 10 October Columbus recorded:

> Here the men could stand it no longer; they complained of the long journey; but the Admiral encouraged them as best he could, holding out good hope of the rewards they could gain. And he added that there was no point in complaining, because he had set out for the Indies and that he intended to persist until he found them, with the help of Our Lord.[3]

This version contrasts with that of those who at a later date gave evidence to the effect that it was Columbus who had wished to turn back and the Pinzón brothers who wished to press on.

Then, on 11 October when the situation had become as serious as it could, there was an increase in flotsam – a piece of wood which looked as though it had been carved with iron was sighted. Once again the hopes of landfall were raised and on the same day, Columbus saw

> a light at ten in the evening on the poop deck, but it was so indistinct that he would not swear that it was land. But he called Pero Gutiérrez, His Majesty's

chamberlain, told him that it seemed to be a light and asked him to look, which he did, and did see it. He also called Rodrigo Sánchez de Segovia, whom the King and Queen had sent as comptroller, and he saw nothing as he was not in a position from which he would see it. After the Admiral had spoken, the light was spotted a couple of times, and it was like a small wax candle being raised and lowered, which struck very few people as being a sign of land, but the Admiral was certain that he was near land . . . [T]he Admiral urged them to keep a good look out from the forecastle and watch for land, saying that he would give the first man to tell him that he could see land a silk doublet, quite apart from the other rewards which the King and Queen had promised, such as the annual payment of ten thousand *maravedís* to the first man to see land.[4]

At 2.00 a.m. the following morning, Friday 12 October 1492, a sailor in the rigging of the *Pinta* sighted land. This sailor, Rodrigo de Triana, claimed the annual pension of 10,000 *maravedís* that the king and queen had promised, but Columbus dismissed the claim and took the reward for himself on the grounds that he had seen land the previous evening and made it over to his abandoned mistress Beatriz.

THREE

THE NEW WORLD

The island in the Bahamas which was Columbus's landfall has never been identified with certainty. Its native name was Guanahaní and Columbus christened it San Salvador. It is the island of this name, known until the 1920s as Watling Island after a pirate, that is widely recognized as the site of the first landing in the New World. Columbus went ashore, had standards planted in the soil and made those with him 'bear witness and testimony that he, in their presence, took possession, as in fact he did take possession, of the said island in the names of the King and Queen'.[1] Nor did he think that the native population should have much say in the fate of their territories, for when, at a later date, he was reporting on his voyage to the Spanish sovereigns, he noted 'many islands filled with people without number, and of them all have I taken possession for their Highnesses by proclamation and with the royal standard displayed, *and nobody objected*' [my italics].[2]

His first contact with the inhabitants of this New World Columbus described thus:

> In order to win their good will, because I could see that they were a people who could more easily be won over and converted to our holy faith by kindness rather than by force, I gave some of them red hats and glass beads that they put round their necks, and many other things of little value, with which they were very pleased and became so friendly that it was a wonder to see.[3]

The offering of holy faith and trinkets was accompanied by some more sinister comments. Columbus noted the natives had wounds on their bodies and understood from the signs they made that enemies came from the mainland with the aim of enslaving them, to which he added the observation, 'they ought to make good slaves . . . [and] would very easily become Christian, for it seemed to me that they had no religion of their own'.[4] He also predicted that it would be very easy to enslave them all because they were so timid. In fact, during these first days he proved remarkably inconsistent in his treatment of the Amerindians. He had seven of them seized and taken aboard the ships with the aim of taking them back to Spain partly as exhibits and partly so they could be taught Spanish. On the other hand, he treated other Amerindians very kindly, feeding them and giving them gifts before letting them go, hoping that they would spread news of the Spaniards' good intentions. It is interesting to note that on 17 October, only five days after Columbus had arrived in the New World, he apparently refers to its inhabitants for the first time as 'Indians', although this may have been a later introduction by Las Casas.

There was, of course, more to the venture than this. Columbus 'watched intently and tried to find out if there was any gold'[5] and observed that the natives wore small gold ornaments in their noses. He was told of a king to the south who had large quantities of the metal, and when the expedition was off Fernandina Island (present Long Island) it was noted that there was a goldfield on it or near it. Likewise Isabela Island (present Crooked Island) was said to have gold because all the natives who came aboard the Spanish ships reported this to be so. The reference in Columbus's *Journal* to finding evidence of gold within hours of reaching the New World is ominous, for it unwittingly set the agenda for European exploration and exploitation in the centuries that followed. The myth of El Dorado belonged to the next century, but it was merely the reification of a dream that drew many across the Atlantic.

From 15 to 23 October Columbus cruised through the Bahamas but expressed a determination to proceed to the mainland and the city of Hangchow so that he might give the sovereigns' letter to the Great Khan. He then learnt of an island which 'if it is as all the Indians of these islands and those I have on the ships say it is, in sign language because I do not understand their tongue, then it is the island of Cipangu of which so many marvellous tales are told'. Indeed, the natives' sign language even conveyed to him the information that the island was 'very large and very busy and . . . there is gold and spices and great ships and merchants'.[6] He sailed off in search of it and reached Cuba on 28 October. At this stage he was still referring to Cuba as an island, but a few days later he abandoned his assumption and concluded that he had reached the mainland of Cathay and that a further large island to the east, Bohío (Hispaniola), was Japan. He even sent an expedition, including the interpreter, into the interior, bearing the sovereigns' letters, to contact the court of the Great Khan, but this enterprise was soon given up when no sign of it could be found.

In making these identifications Columbus was less than rigorous, and indeed his ability to hear in Amerindian names a similarity with those recorded in the Far East by Marco Polo can best be described as a severe case of wishful thinking. Although there were those who distrusted his work, Marco Polo's account of his visit to China in the second half of the thirteenth century was the only one available about that region and extremely popular. Accordingly, Columbus tried to match what Polo reported with what he heard and saw in order to prove that he had visited the same region. It was not simply the similarity of names, such as Cuba for Cathay, but also the information on bizarre social phenomena that could be used for this purpose. For example, when he heard of an island inhabited by a tribe of women without men, an Amazon community, this paralleled exactly the same thing recorded by Marco Polo. Nor, in fact, was it just on his first voyage that he made these connections, for he was still vainly doing it on his fourth voyage, ten years later.

The expedition spent some weeks exploring the northern coast of Cuba with little reward for the the effort expended. The increasing restlessness among the crew worsened when on 20 November Martín Pinzón decamped with the *Pinta* during one of these exploratory trips. It is not clear whether he separated by accident or design, but Columbus had no doubt that it was cupidity and yet a further example of the disloyal and selfish behaviour that he had come to attribute to Pinzón. Stories (from the Amerindians) had now placed the source of gold on a small island to the east, called Babeque (modern Great Inagua) and Columbus feared that Pinzón had gone off to find it on his own. Because of contrary winds, Columbus never reached Babeque but on 5 December he found himself off Bohío, which he christened La Isla Española or Hispaniola (today divided between Haiti and the Dominican Republic).

Columbus's earliest views of the New World expatiated its charms. He described the Bahamas as fertile and green, like an Andalusian spring, and commented on the sweetness of the bird song. But it was for Hispaniola that he kept his most extravagant claims, writing of it to Ferdinand and Isabella in these glowing terms:

> The mountains and hills, the plains and meadow lands are both fertile and beautiful. They are most suitable for planting crops and for raising cattle of all kinds, and there are good sites for building towns and villages. The harbours are incredibly fine and there are many great rivers with broad channels and the majority contain gold. . . . [T]here are many spices and large mines of gold and other metals.[7]

It must be remembered, however, when one reads such a description, that Columbus had every reason to extol the richness of his discoveries.

Hispaniola was inhabited by the Taino Indians who had a sophisticated civilization that shared similarities with those of Meso-America. In his contact with them along the coast, they had proved fearful but once this had been overcome they were friendly, generous and hospitable. This was in direct opposition to the views held of them by neighbouring islanders who claimed that they

ate people, and it is from this early misunder-
standing that originated the word 'cannibal'.
Columbus himself on frequent occasions
expressed scepticism about these reports. On 11
December he wrote (according to Las Casas this is
a verbatim citation):

> Caniba is quite simply the people of the Great Khan
> who must be very close by, and must have ships in
> which they come and capture them, and because
> they do not return they believe that they have been
> eaten.[8]

He even noted that similar accusations had been
made against him and his men. However, this
scepticism did not last long and just over a month
later he was writing of the Caribs that 'they must be
a daring people for they roam these islands eating
anyone they can capture'.[9] Following a skirmish
with Indians on 13 January 1493, the first in the
New World, he immediately assumed the fracas was
with Caribs who were cruel and man-eaters. This
identification of Caribs with fierce, warlike
cannibals has left an unfair smirch on their name –
evidence of their anthropophagy is less than secure
– but justified for the Spaniards a distinction

between friendly and unfriendly Amerindians; the practice made it morally legitimate to enslave the latter.

Sailing along the northern shore of Hispaniola proved very difficult; offshore there were the north-east trades and inshore there were land breezes which only blew at night, a dangerous time to navigate because of the numerous reefs and shoals. It proved too dangerous and in the first minutes of Christmas Day 1492, with the helm left in the care of a boy, the *Santa María* went aground on a sandbank in an ebbing tide. It is indicative of the disloyalty of the crew that the ship's owner and master, Juan de la Cosa, and others who took a boat out with instructions to help free the ship, fled to the *Niña*. Broadside to the sea, the *Santa María* settled on her side, with her seams open but otherwise intact. There was no loss of life and virtually everything of any use on board was saved with the help of the local Amerindians, under the chief, Guancanagarí, who proved very helpful.

To the delight of Columbus and his men, these Amerindians appeared to have considerable quantities of gold. In an abrupt change of plan, perhaps brought about by the fact that one small caravel could not transport everyone back to Europe, Columbus decided to found a colony on the site which he called Puerto Navidad. The duty of those left behind would be to collect gold and locate the mine until a further expedition arrived from Spain to relieve them. Columbus saw in everything that had happened divine intervention; not simply the loss of the ship but even the treachery of those who tried to flee rather than save it, was interpreted as God's wish for the foundation of a settlement. The timbers from the ship were used to build a fort and its guns to arm it, although Columbus thought this was unnecessary because of the cowardice and docility of the natives, but such a construction did display the power of the Spanish crown. It was not difficult to find thirty-nine volunteers to stay because they saw an opportunity to be the first to lay hands on the gold. So certain was Columbus that he was on the verge of finding great wealth that he predicted that by the time he returned there would be such riches that 'the Monarchs would be able in three years to undertake preparations for the conquest of the Holy Land'.[10]

While this was happening, on 27 December news came that the *Pinta* had been sighted on the coast to the east. Columbus, worried that Pinzón would reach Spain and the ears of the monarchs before he did, set out for home in the *Niña* on 4 January 1493. He carried with him a small quantity of gold, assorted natural products and some Indians, although it is not clear how willing they were to travel. On 6 January, Pinzón was sighted and rejoined the expedition. He offered excuses for his behaviour which Columbus privately rejected and publicly accepted. Columbus probably had no alternative as Pinzón almost certainly had the upper hand in terms of support from the crew. Furthermore, whereas he would have liked to complete the exploration of the north coast of Hispaniola, Columbus no longer seemed to have been sufficiently in command to have his way and the relationship between him and Pinzón was very tense. There was nothing left to do except to go home and the two caravels sailed from Hispaniola on 16 January.

A proposed diversion to visit Martinique, which, it was said, was inhabited by Amazon women, was abandoned because of the condition of the ships. A north-easterly course was struck to pick up the westerly winds that would bear them to Europe. By

the second week in February there was considerable
doubt about the ships' exact location, but of the
wildly varying estimates, Columbus's was the most
accurate. Despite the reasons he had given at the
outset of the voyage for falsifying the log, he now
claimed that the reason was 'to mislead the pilots
and sailors who were plotting the course so that he
would remain master of that route to the Indies, as
he in fact remains, because none of the others was
certain of the course and none can be sure of his
route to the Indies'.[11]

Despite navigational problems, all went well until
they ran into a violent storm on 12 February and
the two ships were separated. The storm raged for
three days, and the crew of the *Niña*, with
Columbus on board, vowed to undertake various
pilgrimages if they were saved, drawing lots as to
who would be the person to undertake them. At the
height of the storm and in the middle of the night
Columbus had the first of the mystical experiences
that were to recur in his life at times of crisis. He
was overwhelmed with the fear that he would not
accomplish his mission, that the king and queen
would never get to hear of his great success and
that, as a result, his two sons would become

uncared-for orphans. Against these dismal thoughts he comforted himself with the fact that he was fulfilling God's will and that God, having allowed him to achieve so much, would not now allow him to fail. Just to be on the safe side, he wrote a report of his voyage, wrapped it securely in waxed cloth and then had it cast over the side in a sealed barrel — there is no record of its ever having been retrieved.

On 15 February land was sighted. Although there was much debate, Columbus was correct in identifying it as the Portuguese islands, the Azores. The weather was so bad that it was not until three days later that it was possible to land on Santa María. A part of his crew that went ashore was taken captive and, although they were soon released, it was not until 24 February that they set out again. On leaving the Azores, the *Niña* was caught by another storm that carried it north, back into Portuguese territory at the mouth of the Tagus. Columbus arrived there on 4 March and sent a letter to João II, although he was apprehensive about the welcome he was likely to receive. The Portuguese king invited him to Lisbon, to his court outside the city. The meeting was a difficult encounter as João was trying to find out what

Columbus knew and the latter in turn was trying to conceal it. Columbus revealed enough information for João immediately to claim the discoveries to be Portuguese possessions under the terms of an existing treaty. Columbus responded in a manner that would normally have been a rather dangerous way to treat a monarch, but he survived and was allowed to continue on his journey. He left Lisbon on 13 March and reached Palos two days later, seven-and-a-half months after he had set sail from there.

Until then there had been no sight since mid-February of the *Pinta*, and by coincidence she arrived at Palos a few hours after the *Niña*, having followed a very different route. When the two ships were separated the *Pinta* had missed the Azores and, by accident or design, sailed much further north, making landfall in the small town of Bayona, near Viga in Galicia. As we have seen, the relationship between Columbus and Pinzón was difficult, and there was rivalry between them to claim the honour of the discoveries. On reaching Bayona, Pinzón sent a letter overland to Ferdinand and Isabella, who were in Barcelona, in which he sought permission to come in person to report on the voyage. The monarchs replied in the negative, stating that they wished to hear the news from Christopher Columbus, the commander of the expedition. Following this rebuff, Pinzón turned south, arriving in Palos on the same tide as Columbus. He could not bring himself to enter harbour but had himself put ashore some way out of the town, from where he made his way to his house between Palos and Moguer. A few days later he was dead, but the rivalry between him and Columbus did not die but was continued in the following generations. What story Pinzón would have told if he had survived we do not know, but on the monument to him in Palos he remains described as the real discoverer of America. But it is highly unlikely that Pinzón himself, whatever his navigational skills, could have brought together the political and financial backing that Columbus did and which were essential for such an undertaking.

Columbus moved to Seville and then to Córdoba before being summoned by Ferdinand and Isabella to Barcelona to report in person on his discoveries. He arrived there on 20 April to be fêted and treated almost like royalty. He was confirmed in all the rights and privileges that had formed part of the

Capitulations and granted a coat of arms of great splendour and honour. These months between the first and second crossings saw Columbus at the peak of his career and triumph.

FOUR

THE SECOND CROSSING

There was, however, an outstanding difficulty. Whereas Columbus, as a servant of the Spanish crown, had made these discoveries of land in the west, it was the Pope's right to allot temporal sovereignty to lands not possessed by a Christian ruler. Against a background of rumours concerning the equipping of a large Portuguese expedition, there was intense diplomatic activity. The Spaniards were in a strong position here as Pope Alexander VI was Spanish and had received various favours from Ferdinand and Isabella. The various pronouncements concerning the division of the world that were made during 1493 reflected these circumstances and were unsatisfactory to the Portuguese. King João, whose country was anyway better equipped, decided that it was hopeless to do business with a Spanish pope and approached the Spanish monarchs

Christopher Columbus by Sir
Anthony More. (Hulton Getty)

The 'Montanus' portrait of
Christopher Columbus. It first
appeared in 'Nieuve en
Obekende Weereld', by
Montanus, in 1671; it is thought
to have been painted in
Nuremberg in 1661.
(Hulton Getty)

'The family of Christopher Columbus', from Bryan Edwards, *The History, Civil and Commercial, of the British Colonies in the West Indies* (London, 1801). (Courtesy of the John Carter Brown Library at Brown University)

The 'Talleyrand' portrait of Christopher Columbus, Sebastiano del Piombo (1485?–1547). It was painted after Columbus's death and was owned by the Duke of Valençay de Talleyrand de Sega.
(The Metropolitan Museum of Art, Gift of J. Pierpont Morgan, 1900)

'Columbus argues his case for sailing west to the Indies before the Council of Salamanca', Robert Walter Weir, 1884. (West Point Museum Collection, United States Military Academy)

Anonymous portrait of
Christopher Columbus.
(© Oronoz Fotografos)

Detail from 'La Virgen de
Cristóbal Colón'
(anonymous). (Museo
Lázaro Galdiano)

'The reception of Christopher Columbus by Ferdinand and Isabella',
Eugene Deveria (1808–65).
(Musée Bargoin, Clermont Ferrand, France/Giraudon/Bridgeman Art Library)

Columbus in India primo appellens, magnis exci- IX.
pitur muneribus ab Incolis.

PRIMA *nauigatione, quum Columbus terram attigit, crucem ligneam in littore statuit: deinde prouectus in Hoytin Insulam appellit, quam Hispaniolam nuncupat, & in terram cum multis Hispanis descendit. Ibi quum ab eius loci Cacico (regulum ita appellant) cui nomen Guacanarillo, summa comitate exceptus esset, muneribus inuicem datis & acceptis, ambo sidem amicitiæ futuræ sanxere. Columbus, indusiis, pileolis, cultellis, speculis & similibus eum donauit: Cacicus contra satis magno auri pondere Columbum remuneratus est.*

C 2   *Colum-*

'Columbus in What Was First Called India, Welcomed by the Indians with Gifts',
English School (16th century). This 17th-century print depicts the arrival
of Columbus in the Bahamas.
(Private Collection, Bridgeman Art Library, London/New York)

The coat of arms adopted
by Christopher Columbus
in 1502. (Hulton Getty)

Portrait of Christopher
Columbus, Italian School
(16th century). (Private
Collection/Bridgeman Art
Library, London/New York)

direct. The result was the Treaty of Tordesillas, signed on 7 June 1494. Under its terms all land to the west of a distance of 370 leagues from the Cape Verde Islands (46 degrees, 30 minutes west latitude) would go to Spain regardless of whether it was discovered by a Spaniard or by a Portuguese.

The acceptance of Columbus's discoveries was general and spread quickly throughout Europe. More problematic was confirming what exactly he had discovered. Columbus himself was of the opinion that the lands he had visited were part of Asia, and explicitly stated 'I reached the Indies' to Ferdinand and Isabella. However, there was enough uncertainty to leave room for other views. There were those who agreed with Columbus and they were not proved wrong until 1521 when Magellan revealed the existence of another whole ocean to cross before the Indies were reached. There were those who considered that Columbus had discovered the Antipodes, and those who claimed that he had merely come across more islands of the sort already known, such as the Canaries and the Azores. It was obviously vital for Columbus that Ferdinand and Isabella agree with him but it was not until over a year later that they finally seem to have been persuaded. That there was genuine scepticism that Columbus had opened up a new route to Asia can be seen, as Fernández-Armesto has pointed out, by the lack of commercial upheaval in Italy where the economy depended on established trade routes to the East.

Long before this, in May 1493, only a month after presenting himself to the court in Barcelona, Columbus was commissioned to undertake a second expedition. This was to be on a far grander scale than his first expedition, with the aim of colonization as well as further exploration. In April 1493, Columbus himself prepared a memorandum to the sovereigns in which he proposed a policy for Hispaniola that involved some 2,000 settlers, but the thrust was clearly towards the exploitation of gold and trading, rather than cultivation. The sovereigns responded with their instructions, in which the first and easily the longest paragraph concerned the conversion of the natives to the Christian faith and the good treatment of them. Most of the other paragraphs defined and protected their own rights to the riches that existed. Royal patronage did not cease here, because Columbus's two sons, Diego and Fernando, were transferred to court where they became pages to the heir, Prince Don Juan, until his death in 1497, after which they joined the retinue of Isabella herself.

When it set sail from Cádiz on 25 September, the fleet consisted of seventeen ships, among them the trustworthy *Niña*, and over 1,200 men, including a detachment of twenty cavalry, with, of course, their horses. Although the expedition included farmers and other artisans, it is likely that the volunteers of which the whole party was composed were more attracted to the adventure by the prospect of gold and quick riches than cultivation. Despite the commands of the Spanish monarchs, religious conversion of the native Americans was certainly not a high priority as only two friars and three lay brothers were included. Among those who sailed was Columbus's youngest brother, Diego. No women were included in the party and it would appear that it was not until 1498 that the first European women made the transatlantic crossing.

The expedition was given a great send-off and once again the Canaries and Beatriz de Bobadilla on Gomera were the first port of call. From there a more southerly route than that taken on the first crossing was followed. The journey was rapid and after leaving the Canaries on 13 October Dominica was reached on 3 November. By turning north towards Hispaniola, Columbus was then able to discover in turn the string of islands that form the Lesser Antilles. He also discovered on the first island on which he set foot, Guadeloupe, what seemed to be incontrovertible evidence of cannibalism among the Caribs whom he encountered. One of Ferdinand and Isabella's physicians, Dr Chanca, who accompanied the expedition wrote:

> These people raid the other islands and carry off all the women they can. . . . The Caribs eat the male children they have of them, and only bring up the children of their own women; and as for the men they arc able to capture, they bring those who are alive home to be slaughtered and eat those who are dead on the spot. They say that human flesh is so good that there is nothing like it in the world; and this must be true, for the human bones we found in their houses were so gnawed that no flesh was left on them except what was too tough to be eaten. In one house the neck of a man was found cooking in a pot.[1]

This was both good and bad news. The fierceness of the Caribs suggested that colonization might not be that easy, although this alien practice meant that they could be enslaved without raising any moral difficulties. Furthermore, the existence of cannibals could be taken as further evidence that they were near Asia because ancient sources referred to this behaviour taking place among the peoples of the Far East. On the island of St Croix further traces of cannibalism were found and here the first Spanish death at the hands of Amerindians took place.

After visiting Puerto Rico, the fleet headed for Navidad on Hispaniola's north coast and those who had been left behind the previous year. Even before they arrived there on 28 November, they feared the worst. Four corpses were discovered at the mouth of a river, one of which was in good enough condition for it to have been recognizably bearded and therefore not an Amerindian, who were free of facial hair. Then when the fleet anchored off Navidad there was no response to fire signals and cannon shots. They found the fort burnt to the ground and all thirty-nine Spaniards dead. The Indian chief, Guacanagarí, who claimed that a raiding party of Caribs was responsible, came in for much suspicion, especially when the wound he claimed to have received in fighting them was found not to exist. Another Amerindian version was that the Spaniards had been killed in revenge for the gold and women they stole, and given what we know about later European behaviour this does not seem too unlikely. Guacanagarí was absolved of any guilt and the friendship with him rekindled with presents; instead the natives of the interior were held responsible.

No attempt was made to resurrect the colony at Navidad and instead a new site for settlement was chosen. This, at the mouth of the Rio Bajabonico, was founded on 2 January 1494 and christened Isabela. The location, swampy and unhealthy, was a mistake and the colony never thrived. The men showed little interest in cultivation because gold was their main concern, as it was of their commander. Within three days of landing, expeditions were sent into the interior in search of gold – and when they returned with some gold all the old avaricious dreams were revived. Dr Chanca, writing to the citizens of Seville, revived wild promises: 'On the next voyage which the ships make they will be able to carry away such quantities of gold that anyone who hears of it will be amazed'.[2] When, however, twelve of the seventeen ships left for Spain on 2 February, the report that they carried from Columbus to the monarchs made little reference to any success but included many long demands. Columbus proposed a trade in Carib slaves in order to raise revenue until such time as the goldmines were operational.

On 12 March Columbus made a journey into the interior to inspect the sources of gold for himself. The expedition was equipped to give a display of military might to the inhabitants and a fort, San Tomás, was constructed in order to dominate the area. Columbus arrived back in Isabela on 29 March and almost immediately news came of threats to Fort San Tomás from the native population. A further seventy men were sent to reinforce the garrison of fifty-six; the situation both there and on the coast was bad. Sickness among the Spaniards was rife and many were dissatisfied by the absence of riches, feeling they had been misled. The Amerindians were becoming increasingly troublesome and attempts at revenge by the Spaniards merely served to make matters worse. It was perhaps Columbus's unwillingness to face up to the problems on Hispaniola that persuaded him to go off on further explorations, leaving Diego in charge.

Columbus set out on 24 April with three ships and by the end of the month was exploring the southern coastline of Cuba. He had reassumed the conviction that Cuba was part of mainland Asia and once again the evidence on which he based this assertion, such as the assumed similarity between local names and those mentioned by Marco Polo, suggest he was rather anxious to make this connection. Nor had his willingness to chase other wild geese diminished, and rumours of gold persuaded him to make a side trip to Jamaica. He continued his journey westward along Cuba's coastline but on 12 June, not far from the western extremity (probably at Bahía Cortés) where its insular nature would have revealed itself, Columbus turned back. Before doing so he conducted an extraordinary opinion poll. The crews of all three ships were asked if they had any doubts as to whether this land was the continent of the Indies. Perhaps because they saw no reason to disagree and wished to turn back, no one expressed any doubts, although they were threatened with extraordinary punishment if they were to do so at a later date. The return journey to Isabela against the wind was slow and they did not arrive until 29 September.

Towards the end of the voyage, Columbus was afflicted by 'a high fever and a drowsiness, so that he lost his sight, memory and all his others senses',[3] all of which took him some months to recover from. Nor was there much to cheer him up when he arrived back at Isabela, where the situation if anything had worsened. The one good bit of news was the arrival of his brother, Bartolomé, with three ships. Columbus appointed him *adelantado*, or district governor, an act that was possibly not in his power to do. Although the sovereigns later confirmed the appointment, it had the effect of annoying the colonists who regarded it as an act of favouritism. It thus ultimately proved detrimental to his own interests. A party of discontents mutinied, commandeered Bartolomé's three ships and escaped back to Spain where their stories did Columbus's reputation and career no good. Their complaints and accusations to the monarchs concerned not simply Columbus's behaviour, but also the false promises that he had made about the supplies of gold and other features of the place.

By the end of 1494 the relationship between the Spaniards and the Amerindians had reached a state of open hostility and Columbus seized on this as a way of diverting the complaints against him. He planned a military expedition to subjugate the natives of the interior; this proved to be much more difficult than he had imagined. The campaign, often conducted with brutality, lasted almost a year, but by March 1496, Columbus felt that, through God's providence, peace had been achieved. In fact, although the Amerindians were forced into temporary submission, a lasting peace proved more unrealizable. Just how many of them died as a result of the campaign it is difficult to estimate, but certainly their losses were very high and, despite the fact that the sovereigns had hinted at their disapproval of the enslavement of the Amerindians, this did not stop it taking place. In February 1495 there were 1,600 captive Amerindians of whom perhaps as many as 550 were shipped back to Spain as slaves, the majority falling sick by the time they reached Cádiz. Of the rest, the colonists were allowed to have their pick and the remainder were released. The relations between the natives of the Old and New Worlds had undergone a dramatic change for the worse in less than three years.

While Columbus was thus engaged, Ferdinand and Isabella, in response to the complaints they had received, set up a judicial inquiry into Columbus's discharge of his duties. Such a procedure was quite normal for the time although not usually undertaken until the duty had been discharged. The judicial inspector, Juan Aguado, arrived in Hispaniola in October 1495. Aguado did everything in his power to humiliate Columbus and undermine any authority he had left. As a result Columbus felt he had no alternative but to return to Spain to fight his corner at the royal court. He, with many others sick of the New World, left Isabela, a rapidly dying city, in March 1496 and arrived back in Cádiz in June.

His second return was not accompanied by the welcome he had received on his first. His reaction was that his misfortune was the result of pride, and he adopted the role of penitent, appearing in public in a Franciscan robe with unkempt hair and beard. He wrote to the sovereigns who replied the following month, saying that they would see him when he felt well enough to travel to Burgos in the north of the country. The audience took place in October and Columbus, forever the optimist, thought it went well. In fact, it was not very successful and there was much hostility towards him at court. The words of disaffected colonists were having their effect and it was said that he was a bad governor, an ineffective leader and even a poor navigator who dangerously pursued dreams and mirages. His failure to make any progress in opening up a route to the Indies, if that indeed was where he was heading, had encouraged his enemies and increased the level of criticism against him. Ferdinand and Isabella no doubt appreciated the degree to which such hostility was likely to be the product of jealousy, but it is equally likely that they would have noticed that Columbus always claimed to be right and had a tendency to fall out with people.

Columbus was to spend the next two years in Spain trying to convince his royal patrons of the merits of mounting a third expedition. He prepared memoranda for the sovereigns on matters concerning the governance, settlement, religious arrangements and economic development of the Indies. He wrote further memoranda proposing a crusade against Mecca and a trading visit to Calicut, the destination of Vasco da Gama's voyage currently being fitted out in Portugal. Indeed, it seems to have been geopolitical considerations that carried the day. King João of Portugal was known to believe that there existed a continent to the west, directly opposite southern Africa. Columbus himself had heard from his native informants similar stories of a large land mass to the south. The important question to be answered was whether, under the terms of the Treaty of Tordesillas, this land fell in the Spanish or Portuguese sphere of influence. The answer was to go and find out, and this, in part, was the aim of Columbus's third voyage. Restored to the monarchs' favour and reconfirmed as viceroy and governor of the Indies, Columbus received permission early in 1498 to go ahead.

FIVE

THE THIRD CROSSING

Columbus sailed from Sanlúcar de Barrameda at the mouth of the Guadalquivir in late May 1498. His fleet consisted of six ships, and after stops at Madeira and the Canary Islands half the ships headed straight for Hispaniola, while Columbus went exploring with the other three ships. The course he took this time was much more southerly, sailing down the coast of Africa as far as the Cape Verde Islands before heading west. The good relations existing between Spain and Portugal at the time allowed such a detour and although one reason for doing this, as we have seen, was to investigate the existence of an antipodean continent there may have been another. The Portuguese had found gold in Africa at this latitude, and the given wisdom of the time, derived from Aristotle, was that similar products, including minerals, were to be found at the same latitude and it was believed that gold was at its most abundant in the equatorial regions.

Columbus left the Cape Verde Islands on 1 July but within two weeks he found himself becalmed in the doldrums, that windless region between the north-east and south-east trade winds. Las Casas recorded this dramatic account of the experience from Columbus's journal:

> . . . he came into such great vehement, burning heat that he feared lest the ships catch fire and the people perish. . . . [N]o one would dare to go below to look after the casks of wine and water, which burst, snapping the hoops of the pipes; the wheat burned like fire; the bacon and salt meat roasted and putrified.[1]

After eight days of this an unseasonable south-east breeze allowed him to escape. When only a couple of days' sailing from the South American coastline, somewhere in the region of modern Guyana, he turned north-west and on 31 July sighted three mountain peaks on what has ever since been known as the island of Trinidad. He approached from the south-east, making landfall at the present Galeota Point, and cruised westward along the southern shoreline to the Serpent's Mouth, the channel between Trinidad and the South American landmass that has retained the name that Columbus gave it. Indeed, it was on 1 August 1498 that the first sighting of the continent was made, although it was assumed to be merely another island.

The fleet passed through the Serpent's Mouth into the Gulf of Paria before it became obvious that the violence of the current passing through the channel would make it very difficult to return that way. Accordingly, they continued north, banking on a way out in that direction. On 4 August, the peninsula of Paria was reached and the following day the first Spaniards set foot on mainland America although, at the time, it was assumed to be another island. Exploration further west continued until 11 August when the northernmost mouths of the Orinoco River were found. At the time it did not seem to have occurred to anyone that the existence of this vast freshwater river must be indicative of a huge landmass. The expedition then turned back and sailing north through the Dragon's Mouth, another of Columbus's names, the northern shore of the Paria Peninsula was explored, until

15 August, when, in the region of the island of Margarita, it was decided to turn north for Hispaniola. This was a curious moment to do so since the Amerindians of the peninsula had all indicated that this was the area where the pearls which they possessed originated. Unlike the mythical gold mines, the pearl beds were very much a reality that duly yielded up great wealth. Columbus must have also felt that his sudden decision needed some explanation and in a letter to the sovereigns listed six excuses for his action, which ranged from the need to get the supplies he had on board to Hispaniola before they all rotted, that he had the wrong sort of vessels for coastal exploration and that he was sick with the eye complaint that had plagued him four years earlier when off Cuba.

It was at this point also that Columbus decided that Paria was not an island and he wrote in his journal, 'I have come to believe that this is a mighty continent which was hitherto unknown'.[2] Although the existence of an antipodean land mass had been hypothesized by past scholars, it is to Columbus that the credit must go for empirically confirming its existence and recognizing it for what it is.

Indeed, he came to appreciate that a river the size of the Orinoco could only flow from a large continent, although in reports to the sovereigns he hedged his bets. 'I say that if this river does not originate in the Terrestrial Paradise, it comes and flows from a land of infinite size to the south, of which we have no knowledge.'[3] Columbus half-suspected that it was no ordinary landmass for on it he located the Terrestrial Paradise, the Garden of Eden whence God had ejected Adam and Eve. His evidence for this was the assumption that paradise lay at the end of the Orient, which was where Columbus judged himself to be, that it was the source of mighty rivers and had a temperate climate. That was not all, for he misinterpreted certain astronomical observations of the pole star from which he concluded that they had been sailing uphill. This could only mean that the earth

. . . does not have the kind of sphericity described by the authorities, but that it has the shape of a pear, which is all very round, except at the stem, which is rather prominent, or that it is as if one had a very round ball, on one part of which something like a woman's teat were placed, this part with the stem being the uppermost and nearest the sky, lying below

the equinoctial line in this ocean sea, at the end of
the East.[4]

In other words, Paria was on this bulge of the
earth's surface and over the horizon to the south lay
the Terrestrial Paradise. Not surprisingly this radical
new theory about the world's shape received a
rather sceptical response, but one must remember
that Columbus was trying to fit his observations
with a set of medieval notions still heavily
influenced by scriptural authority.

Columbus arrived at Santo Domingo on
31 August. This city, the capital of today's
Dominican Republic, which had been founded in
July 1496 at the mouth of the River Ozama on the
southern coast of Hispaniola, was the first successful
European settlement in the New World. It was the
result of instructions to Bartolomé to abandon the
doomed settlement of Isabela and find a suitable site
for a new colony. Columbus's journey from
Margarita to Santo Domingo is often held up as an
example of his outstanding intuition as a navigator.
When he left Margarita on 15 August it had been
over six weeks since he had sailed from the Cape
Verde Islands and reference has already been made

to the hit-and-miss science of navigation at the time. Even so, Columbus, sailing among the currents of a totally unknown sea, made landfall in Hispaniola only 100 miles from his destination. Perhaps it was luck on this occasion.

If, as far as the location of the colony was concerned, things were much improved, nothing else was. Relations with the native population were bad, and many of the Spaniards were deeply dissatisfied with their circumstances as a result of a sharp difference between expectations and reality; for the colonists the former were based on the exaggerated promises of wealth and ease that Columbus had made, whereas the latter was characterized by an unpleasant environment, difficult natives and hard work. Much of the resentment, accordingly, was focused on Columbus and his brothers. Francisco Roldán, the chief justice, had proposed removing all restrictions on individual goldmining and use of Indian labour, and had led a mutiny with about 100 followers. Bartolomé had managed to contain the uprising but then the three ships with supplies that Columbus had despatched from the Canary Islands overshot Santo Domingo, fell into the mutineers' hands and gave them fresh impetus. On arrival Columbus tried to assert his authority by force but on discovering that he had little support, he attempted reconciliation instead. The outcome was that Roldán more or less dictated his own terms and Columbus's position was close to surrender. One of these terms was that all those who wanted to return home should be offered a free passage. The consequence of this was that a new wave of anti-Columbus stories spread through Spain; it was said of Columbus and Bartolomé that they were 'always quick to torture, hang and behead'. Fernando Colón was to give this account of the accusations made against them:

> . . . they were cruel and unfit to govern because they were foreigners and had no experience of governing men of quality. These rebels declared that if their Highnesses did not intervene, it would lead to the total ruin of the Indies. And if ruin were avoided, the Admiral would in time rebel and form an alliance with some foreign prince, claiming the Indies were his own possession because he had discovered them by his own efforts and industry. That, they said, was why the Admiral sought to conceal the wealth of that country and did not allow the Indians to serve the Christians or be converted to our faith, hoping

thereby to win them to his side and use them against
their Highnesses.[5]

Columbus had barely achieved some sort of
peace with Roldán when he was confronted with a
more serious situation. In September 1499, Alonso
de Hojeda, a former ally of Columbus, arrived in
Hispaniola and threw in his lot with the surviving
bands of rebels. Hojeda had obtained permission
from the Spanish monarchs to search for the pearls
that Columbus had reported off the Venezuelan
coast. That such permission had been given is
indicative of how hostile to Columbus the
atmosphere in court must have turned as it was to
all intents and purposes a trespass on his monopoly
on transatlantic commerce. Columbus left Roldán
to deal with this new problem as he had more or
less surrendered authority to him in the south of the
island. But this was but one of a whole series of
uprisings both on the part of malcontent Spaniards
and maltreated Amerindians, all of which
underlined the chaos in which the colony found
itself.

It was clear that things could not go on like this
and at this juncture Columbus made an odd and ill-

advised request to his sovereigns; he said he needed help and asked them to provide him with a knowledgeable administrator of justice. It is not clear what he expected but he got more than he bargained for. The monarchs appointed Francisco de Bobadilla (not apparently related to Columbus's friend on Gomera) with 'supreme judiciary powers'. Bobadilla, of ancient Spanish nobility, was a loyal and trusted servant of the crown who was not friendly towards Columbus. When he arrived in Santo Domingo he apparently found displayed the corpses of two recently hanged Spaniards, Diego in charge and Columbus and Bartolomé away putting down another revolt. Diego refused to surrender his charge and Bobadilla had him put in chains. When Columbus and Bartolomé returned, a similar fate befell them after they refused to acknowledge Bobadilla's authority and the three of them were sent back to Spain. Bobadilla, in the meantime, confiscated for his own use Columbus's property.

Columbus put his chains to good use. On the voyage back to Spain in October 1500, the captain of the ship suggested that he might remove them but Columbus refused to do so for 'he was resolved to keep those chains as a memorial of how well he had been rewarded for his many services. And this he did, for I [Fernando Colón] always saw them in his bedroom, and he wanted them buried with his bones.'[6] This ploy worked, for back in Cádiz and Seville he flaunted them in the streets until Ferdinand and Isabella, hearing of it and thinking that Bobadilla had overstepped the mark in his harsh treatment of Columbus, sent a message ordering him to be set free (one version has it that he actually appeared with his chains in the royal presence). It may be for the same reason that Columbus was not kept waiting long for a royal audience. He, together with his two brothers, appeared before the monarchs in December, and Columbus called for reparation and revenge. The monarchs agreed in principle to the restoration of his goods, rights and privileges but nothing was actually done. Optimistic as ever, and buoyed up by faith in his divine purpose, Columbus was confident that he would be reinstated and began to put together a more systematic appraisal of how much of his divine purpose he had fulfilled and what remained to be done. By careful examination of the Scriptures he identified those achievements for which he could claim credit and those left for him to do. At this point Columbus reactivated the scheme which he had proposed before his first crossing and of which he never lost sight – the restoration of Jerusalem to Christian control. He accumulated his findings in what is known as *The Book of Prophecies*, which he sent to Ferdinand and Isabella, but it is not clear whether either monarch ever looked at this work.

Columbus's optimism must have suffered a blow when in September 1501 the efficent and reliable Don Nicolás de Ovando was appointed governor-general of Hispaniola, a post which Columbus himself claimed by right of the agreement that he had orignally struck with Ferdinand and Isabella. Despite this setback his fortunes revived over the winter of 1501–2, and he managed to raise money from Genoese sources in order to promote his right to trade with the lands he had discovered. Up until then, the crown's policy of licensing others to continue the exploration on the other side of the Atlantic – a monopoly that Columbus regarded as his – had yielded only a small profit and discovered little of significance. The exception to this was to the south where in January 1500 Vicente Yáñez Pinzón reached Brazil, although this discovery was of no advantage to Spain as it lay on the Portuguese side of the Tordesillas line and thus gave Portugal a foothold in the New World. Columbus may have realized that he might be able to take advantage of the relative failure of his rivals and reinstate himself by fulfilling his dream of reaching the Indies that had so far eluded him. At about the time that Ovando left to take up his office in Hispaniola in February 1502, Columbus petitioned the sovereigns for permission to make a further voyage of discovery. The sovereigns replied with remarkable speed to Columbus's request and wrote on 14 March granting permission and issuing instructions. What is interesting is the insistence in the sovereigns' two communications that Columbus was not to delay his departure: 'you should leave at once without any delay', and again 'you must set sail with your vessels as speedily as may be'.[7] It has been suggested that Ferdinand and Isabella could not wait to see the back of the importunate Columbus.

The monarchs added their regret that he had been imprisoned and his goods confiscated, but assured him that they would be restored. Columbus was instructed not to go near Hispaniola on his outward voyage and only to visit it briefly on his return. The instructions also contained a very explicit order not to take slaves, although this injunction was rather weakened by the qualification that it was all right to return with Amerindians if they wished to come of their own accord.

SIX

THE FOURTH CROSSING

Columbus set out on his fourth and last crossing of the Atlantic on 3 April 1502, his fleet composed of four caravels. There was a strong family presence as both his brother, Bartolomé, and his thirteen-year-old son, Fernando, accompanied him. His orders were simple: he was to pick up the exploration of the mainland from where he had left off on his third voyage. He had not given up his original idea of finding a western sea route to the East. Even if recent explorations had increasingly indicated large land masses to north and south, Columbus remained convinced that he would be able to continue west by sea at the latitude of his earlier explorations. Indeed he fully expected to meet Vasco da Gama who was on his second voyage to the East, and the monarchs of Spain and Portugal directed their respective subjects to treat each other as friends when they met.

By now Columbus had the Atlantic crossing down to a fine art, and it took just twenty-one days from the Canaries to Martinique, where he arrived on 15 June. As has been mentioned Columbus had been forbidden to visit Hispaniola, but his loss of governorship which he regarded as a breach of contract rankled and he had considerable pecuniary interest in the colony. Whatever the reason, and the excuse he gave was that one of his ships was unseaworthy, he disobeyed his orders and arrived off Hispaniola on 29 June and asked permission to enter the harbour of Santo Domingo. There was some urgency to his request as he had noted the signs of an approaching hurricane, but Ovando refused him shelter and did not listen to his storm warning. While Columbus's ships found haven in a small bay along the coast, the main fleet that had brought Ovando was allowed to depart for home. It was caught in the hurricane and nineteen ships were lost, over 500 men drowned including Columbus's enemies, Bobadilla who had arrested him and sent him home in chains and the rebel

Roldán. Reputedly the single ship that made it back to Spain was carrying part of Columbus's own property.

Whatever divine justice Columbus may have thought he had been served, from then on his luck ran out and nothing went right for him. His northerly route via Hispaniola made the original plan to explore westward along the Paria coast from the point he had reached in 1498 impractical because of the adverse winds and currents. Instead he headed west, passing Cuba and making landfall at the present island of Guanaja, off Cape Honduras, on 30 July. It was immediately observable that the inhabitants of this island and the neighbouring mainland had a more developed way of life than the people of the Caribbean islands; in particular their technology was more advanced with knowledge of metal smelting. Columbus had brushed up against the fringes of the Meso-American civilizations, and had he followed the coast westward he might well have found them seventeen years before Cortés. Instead, he turned east and a little down the coast at Rio de la Posesión he went ashore to claim the land in the names of the King and Queen of Spain. Continuing eastward, the expedition had to endure almost four weeks of foul weather in which the ships were damaged, stores lost and the morale of the crew fell. Columbus was by no means free of anxiety and self-pity. In a letter to Ferdinand and Isabella, he wrote of his concern for the sufferings of his crew and his kinsmen, and continued, 'As for myself I had won little profit in twenty years of toilful and dangerous service, for today in Castile I have no roof to shelter me. When I want a meal or a bed I must go to an inn or tavern, and more often than not I have not the money to pay the bill.'[1]

Progress was very slow and by 14 September the fleet had only reached Cape Gracias a Dios, a distance of under 200 miles. At this point, on the border between present-day Honduras and Nicaragua, the coastline turned south and the weather improved. By 25 September the present site of Puerto Limón, in Costa Rica, was reached and by 6 October the fleet was anchored in the Chiriquí Lagoon in Panama. Here contact was made with the Guaymi Indians from whom Columbus learnt of a large sea and a state called

Ciguare, where, he was told, there were ships with cannon and horses. Even if make-believe, this report was enough on which to base the assumption that this was Ciambu, the Cochin-China of Marco Polo, and that the Ganges was only ten days away. Indeed Columbus assumed that he had reached the longitude of eastern China, and was travelling down the Malay Peninsula.

The fleet then continued eastward along an inhospitable coast, first to Veragua and then on to Nombre de Dios, much of the last part of the journey the unintended effect of a storm. From there, on 23 November, Columbus turned back to Veragua, but the constantly contrary winds and currents meant that it was not until 6 January 1503, having spent Christmas and New Year near where the entrance to the Panama Canal now is, that he was in the vicinity of that river. He made his base from which to explore for gold in the interior at the mouth of a river christened Belén, a little to the east of Veragua. Exploration revealed gold in the interior in greater quantities than elsewhere in the New World. Columbus decided to build a township there and to leave his brother in charge of a party of the men while he went to obtain help for its exploitation. The settlement of Santa María de Belén had been constructed and the three ships were ready to depart when it was found that the water level had dropped so far that there was no longer sufficient depth to clear the bar at the mouth of the river. Coincidental with this was a sharp deterioration in the relationship between the Spaniards and the Guaymi, brought about as usual by the former's treatment of the latter. A large war party assembled and although the Spaniards made a pre-emptive strike and took hostages, Columbus could not have forgotten the fate of Navidad. Even so, with a rise in the water level, the three ships scheduled to leave managed to cross the bar. The situation then deteriorated further and attacks by the Guaymi killed a number of the Spaniards. The colony and the ship still in the river were abandoned.

It was during this period of high tension that Columbus, in the depth of despair, had another of his divine experiences. He heard a voice which said to him, 'O fool, slow to believe and serve thy God, the God of all! What more did he do for Moses or David his servants than he has done for thee?', and ended with the words, 'Fear not, have trust, all these tribulations are inscribed on marble and are not purposeless.'[2]

The condition of the ships was rapidly deteriorating as their timbers had become so infested with boring worms that they were taking on water as fast as it could be pumped out. Columbus decided that the only escape route was back to Hispaniola and they set out on 16 April, travelling east along the coast in order to be to the windward of Santo Domingo before turning north. Severe weather added to their problems and on 23 April one of the ships, no longer seaworthy, had to be abandoned. A navigational mistake, not Columbus's, resulted in their turning north too soon and arriving at Cuba, leaving the expedition with the difficult task of working their way eastward along the coast against wind and current. During the last open-sea voyage, between Cuba and Hispaniola, the ships, now barely afloat, were blown off course towards Jamaica. The site of the first landfall proved unsuitable through lack of fresh water and the ships, no longer fit to go further, were moved a few miles down the coast to the present St Ann's Bay. Here they were run aground, shored upright and thatched huts constructed on their decks; they became to all intents and purposes glorified houseboats.

The 116 men found themselves castaways, without provisions and with virtually no chance of being found. The first step was to organize a supply of food and this task was given to Diego Méndez, a loyal follower of Columbus, who successfully arranged this with various native villages. When a call was made for volunteers to try to reach Hispaniola to obtain help, it was once again Méndez who took on the task. He modified a small local canoe to make it more seaworthy and with one other European and six natives he set out early in July. Méndez carried with him a letter to the Spanish sovereigns requesting that they send a ship and provisions to rescue the expedition. The first attempt was turned back by hostile Indians, but the second, consisting of two canoes, each with six Europeans and ten Amerindians, and escorted by an armed guard until they left Jamaica, was successful in reaching

Hispaniola. The idea of sending two canoes was so that one could return to inform those left behind that the passage had been successfully accomplished and that rescue could be expected. However, the commander of the second canoe could not find anyone, European or Amerindian, willing to make the return journey. One can well understand the reluctance of the Europeans, but the case of the Amerindians is more surprising especially given their extensive navigation of the Caribbean. Méndez set off along the coast, but before he reached Santo Domingo he heard that the governor, Ovando, was on a campaign subduing the natives of the interior and went to find him there. Ovando was not displeased at the news of Columbus's misfortune and did nothing to expedite Méndez's mission. Accordingly it was not until March 1504 that Méndez reached Santo Domingo to organize a rescue.

In the meantime Columbus was faced with trouble from both Europeans and Amerindians. Knowing how in the past the behaviour of his men had antagonized the local population, Columbus had more or less confined them to the ships. As time went by and nothing seemed to happen, there was increasing discontent until 2 January 1504, when forty-eight men, about half the expedition, led by the brothers Francisco and Diego de Porras, revolted, seized some canoes, abducted some natives to act as crew and tried to escape to Hispaniola. The attempt failed and the mutineers made their way back overland towards St Ann's Bay. It is not clear whether it was the result of the abusive treatment that the Amerindians received at the mutineers' hands but about this time the supply of food to those who had remained loyal started to dry up. In an event predictive of the later more famous fictional incident in Rider Haggard's *King Solomon's Mines*, Columbus threatened that on 29 February 1504 the moon would be devoured unless the natives continued to bring food. Columbus's prediction of the full eclipse, obtained from an astronomical almanac he had with him, so impressed the natives that trouble in that quarter dissipated and supplies were renewed.

Soon after this occurrence a violent clash took place between the loyalists and the mutineers from which the former emerged triumphant. The

Porras brothers were put in irons and their followers surrendered. At the same time a small caravel sent by Ovando arrived, not to pick up Columbus and his men but to check on their circumstances. The captain of this vessel provided the castaways with two casks of wine, a side of salt pork and the valuable news that Méndez was organizing a rescue. Except for this small caravel there were no ships in Santo Domingo and Méndez had had to wait for ships to arrive from Spain before he could hire a vessel to rescue Columbus's party. This did not happen until June 1504, and it was on 29 June, over a year after arriving on Jamaica, that the party finally left. The journey back to Santo Domingo was painfully slow, lasting until 13 August. Ovando expressed his pleasure at Columbus's safe delivery, but the fact that he released the Porras brothers was perhaps a better indicator of his feelings.

Columbus did not delay in Santo Domingo and a month later, on 12 September, he left his New World for the last time. The final transatlantic journey was rough and slow, the vessel being dismasted in a violent storm. San Lúcar was not reached until 7 November, after a voyage of fifty-six days.

SEVEN

THE END

The fourth voyage can be claimed as both a success and failure. Columbus had certainly failed once again to find a route to the Indies, but on the other hand he had greatly extended his earlier discoveries and located gold in quantities not previously found in the New World. There was certainly no rapturous welcome and no order to attend at court. Indeed, it would have been surprising if there had been, as Columbus arrived back in Spain just nineteen days before the death of Queen Isabella, who had been in declining health for over a year. This was a blow to Columbus who had always seen her as his particular patron, rather than the king, whom he had always found somewhat abrupt and unenthusiastic about his plans. Even so, he initially entertained some hope that Ferdinand would restore to him his governorship of

Hispaniola and all the privileges and titles which he believed were owed to him. This optimism quickly gave way to the belief that the king was actively antagonistic towards him and that he was intending to deprive him and his heirs of his rightful dues on the grounds that the original agreement had been too generous. Columbus, for his part, regarded himself as literally heaven-sent to the crowns of Spain, who should be more grateful.

During the winter of 1504–5, Columbus was in Seville and indisposed for much of the time with severe gout, able only to get about on a litter. He was relatively rich although he did not see it that way. He felt that he had been cheated of much that was due to him under the *Capitulations*. He had not received 10 per cent of the riches of the lands he had discovered but only 10 per cent of the sovereigns' fifth, in other words 2 per cent. It is also unlikely that he ever received the eighth of the profit on his own ventures in the New World. Less justifiable was his complaint that he had not been paid one-third of the tax on the trade with places under his jurisdiction, but this was a claim that he made in his *Book of Privileges* even though the payment had never been sanctioned.

In May 1505, Columbus felt well enough to travel to court which was then in Segovía. His interview with the king was not a success and Columbus's claims that he had been sent by God, reference to his past opportunities to work for other royal patrons and his promise to make even more glorious discoveries were not likely to have endeared him to Ferdinand. Despite continued bad health, Columbus trailed round after the court, first to Salamanca and then Valladolid. He never gave up and in April 1506 Columbus addressed the newly arrived successors to Isabella on the throne of Castile, her daughter Juana and her husband Felipe, with a plea that the honour and estate as promised in the terms of his commission be restored to him. Not long after this, and probably on 20 May 1506, Columbus died in Valladolid.

Death did not bring a close to Columbus's travels. He was initially buried in the Church of San Francisco in Valladolid, but in 1509 his remains were transferred, on the orders of his brother Diego, to a chapel in the monastery of Las

Cuevas, across the Guadalquivir from Seville, where Columbus had spend much of his time between his third and fourth voyages. In 1541 they were then transferred, together with those of his brother Bartolomé and his son Diego, to the cathedral in Santo Domingo, where they were interred in front of the high altar. Here they stayed until the French occupation of the country in 1795, when they were moved again, this time to Havana. In 1898, when Cuba obtained its independence from Spain, the remains travelled back across the Atlantic for interment in Seville Cathedral.

At least, that is the most widely held view, although with all the toing and froing there is scope for an alternative claim. It is founded on the discovery in 1877, while repairs were being done to Santo Domingo Cathedral, of a coffin marked inside and out as being that of Admiral Christopher Columbus. The Dominican Republic remains convinced that these are the genuine remains of Columbus and as part of the five hundredth anniversary celebrations in 1992 the government constructed the vast Faro a Colón (Columbus lighthouse) in the shape of a cross, as well as installing at the transept a magnificent sepulchre, permanently guarded by an armed escort of marines.

One of Columbus's constant fears was that the right of his heirs to succeed to his titles and privileges, as laid down in the *Capitulations*, would not be recognized and that the dynasty it was his ambition to found would die with him. In the short term his worries were unfounded and in hindsight the king proved anything but hostile to Columbus and his family. He made sound provision for Diego, who had been brought up at the royal court. He permitted his marriage to María de Toledo, a cousin of the king, and made him governor of Santo Domingo in 1509, where Diego proved a competent administrator of the arrangements that Ovando had put in place. Diego died in 1526 and was succeeded by his worthless son, Luis. Fernando, on the other hand, had become a scholar and had put together an outstanding library. He lived to 1539, long enough to see what his father had feared, for in 1536 the Council of the Indies ruled that Columbus's heirs should forego the title of viceroy and all revenues in exchange for the

Duchy of Veragua (in present-day Panama where Columbus had been in 1502–3) and an annual pension in perpetuity. The widowed María de Toledo accepted these conditions on behalf of her son, Luis.

EIGHT

RETROSPECT

A recent biography of Columbus starts with the words 'Considered from one point of view, Columbus was a crank.'[1] One can well see that many of his contemporaries might have held that opinion, and if he had not reached the Americas in 1492 or not returned from his journey he would have disappeared from the historical record as many other cranks must have done. Crank or not, Columbus, like so many other individuals of remarkable achievement, was a complex character and not the most comfortable person to live with. On the other hand it is probably true to say that it is just these failings, which from another point of view might be regarded as virtues, that drove him to achieve what he did. Perhaps that is the most important point to make. Whatever his detractors, and there is no lack of them, say about him – that he was not the first European to visit the Americas; or that he did not know what he was doing; or that he knew very well what he was doing; or that he was responsible for initiating the greatest demographic disaster that the world has experienced – they cannot really diminish what was an amazing feat and one which can only have been repeated a limited number of times in the history of humankind. It is also the only one of which we have any kind of written record.

The history of humanity has been one of exploration, first of the surface of the world and within the last half of the twentieth century, of space. Until 500 years ago, most of this exploration was on or in sight of land. This, of course, did not mean that it was not a hazardous undertaking, but the crucial component of uncertainty was missing. You may not have known exactly where you were or where you were going, but the psychological impact of this is very different when one is in the middle of the ocean with an unbroken horizon, and nothing except yourself and those people and things you have with you. The modern-day equivalent would be to have blasted the first manned rocket into space without any radio contact, no accurate navigational equipment, only assumptions about the destination, and no certain means of return. There is no suggestion here that Columbus and his men thought they were going to fall off the edge of the world; it has already been made clear that it was generally recognized that the world was round, not flat, and Columbus definitely thought he would reach somewhere, if not the Indies, by going west. That Columbus selected those bits of existing geographical knowledge that represented his project in the most favourable light is not too surprising; he would have been silly to have done otherwise. The problem was that his undercalculation of the circumference of the globe just did not convince the various commissions of enquiry that were asked to look at his plans. The unexplained matter is what exactly happened between the apparently final rejection of his proposal in January 1492 and the almost instant decision to allow him to go ahead. The answer is almost certainly that the evidence of experts is often ignored in favour of economics, politics and self-interest, and Columbus had been clever enough to surround himself with powerful friends.

This fact is important in trying to understand Columbus, for one should not overlook his personal qualities. He arrived in the Iberian Peninsula as a man of no importance or status, and within relatively few years had built up a remarkable network of influential people. He must have been very persuasive, even if at times too much so. Certainly the impression is given that in 1502, in granting permission for the fourth voyage, Ferdinand and Isabella could not wait to see him depart and thus be free of his importuning. It is also clear that whereas Columbus had an aptitude for making friends he was equally good at turning them into enemies. That he made enemies is not surprising; to go from nothing to the triumph of his return in 1493, with all the wealth and honours that he could claim, was likely to have aroused a great deal of jealousy. Even the sovereigns must have realized that the deal they had struck with him had had the unforeseen result of potentially creating a far richer and more powerful individual than they had dreamt of. In a way they were saved from fulfilling their side of the bargain as a result of Columbus's singular failure properly to administer and control the territory of which they had appointed him governor-general and viceroy.

One of the questions that has always surrounded Columbus's first voyage was how he came to find, at his first attempt, nearly the best route across the Atlantic. The anti-Columbus answer has tended to be because when he set out across the Atlantic he must have known where he was going and how to get there – otherwise how would he have known to go south to the latitude of the Canary Islands and pick up the trade winds before turning west? The response to such objections is that by the end of the fifteenth century people had had experience of sailing off the African Atlantic coast for many decades and Columbus himself was acquainted with those seas. In other words, it could barely have escaped the attention of mariners that there is at those latitudes a wind that blows steadily from east to west. The same can be said about the return voyage and it is difficult to accept that Columbus turned northwards, and thus picked up the westerlies, purely by chance, as anyone who sailed in the North Atlantic must have been fully aware that the prevailing winds there are from that direction. In other words, finding the best route across the Atlantic and back was partly a matter of good observation and the application of practical knowledge. But this leaves open the question of how good a navigator Columbus was.

This is difficult to judge. He often portrays himself or is portrayed by his son as being accurate in his calculations when others have made mistakes. For example, on his first return voyage he correctly calculated the ship's position as near the Azores which it turned out to be, whereas others were wildly inaccurate in their estimates. But then, of course, Columbus is the source of this account. On the other hand, he often got things profoundly wrong. What can be said for him is that he was observant and learnt quickly. His realization that the pole star moves and his recognition of the signs of an approaching hurricane off Santo Domingo in 1502 are evidence of that. This was also a contemporary view, for Michele De Cuneo, a Genoese adventurer who accompanied the second expedition, wrote of him:

no other man has been born so . . . keen in practical navigation as the above-mentioned Lord Admiral; for when navigating, only by looking at a cloud or by night at a star, he knew what was going to happen and whether there would be foul weather.[2]

It is questionable whether anyone at the end of the fifteenth century, and for some further centuries, could be a good navigator if we judge such competence in terms of locating oneself by accurate measurements. The instruments were not available to take such measurements and the whole business was inevitably hit-and-miss direct reckoning. If we forget for a minute Columbus's transatlantic voyages and concentrate on those in the Caribbean, some picture of his skill emerges. Admittedly, the Caribbean may appear a rather insignificant stretch of water compared with the Atlantic Ocean, but sailing it presents its own difficulties. Columbus had to cope with storms, currents, variable winds and shoals, all of them uncharted and about none of which he would have had prior information. It is true that *Santa María* ran aground and was lost, but that was barely his fault — even the most conscientious captain has to sleep sometime and Columbus did more than his share of staying awake to keep watch. He lost all the vessels on his fourth expedition through failure to careen them, which may be classed as careless seamanship but not bad navigation. His is a truly remarkable record and he cannot have endlessly relied on others throughout his career of exploration; some, if not all, of the honour for his remarkable feats of exploration, is due to Columbus.

How much of the efforts to detract from his achievements are the result of other factors, either his personal failings or the hostility of others? Columbus is often depicted as a man of extreme arrogance who saw himself as an instrument of God's will; as a man of burning ambition determined to load himself with riches and titles that would found a dynasty; as a man deeply suspicious of others' motives (often, one imagines, quite rightly) and thus unable to form lasting friendships and alliances. Many of those with whom he worked closely turned against him at a later date. The exceptions to this were his brothers, Bartolomé and Diego, on whom he came increasingly to rely and to whom he delegated considerable authority. This in itself may have been a mistake as it made it easy to portray the Columbus family as a group of self-interested Genoese whose loyalty to Spain was questionable. There is probably some truth in all of this, and the impression that often comes across is of someone who, if he had been politically more astute, might well have avoided much of the hostility that confronted him.

The alternative picture is of a visionary who had the strength of mind and purpose to achieve what he did in the face of lesser mortals determined to obstruct him; a man to whom divine voices spoke directly; a hero who made the most dramatic discovery of all time and changed the face of the globe; and a man who had to struggle to receive the rewards he had been promised and the recognition he deserved. These two views are not necessarily contradictory, and indeed are the kinds of reactions that the reputation of any great historical figure has to face. History will go on judging Columbus in these contrasting ways and even if further evidence concerning his life were to surface, it is unlikely that it would be conclusive one way or the other. Of one thing it is possible to be certain: Columbus and what he did will not be forgotten.

NOTES

INTRODUCTION

1. Fernando Colón, *The Life of Christopher Columbus* (Folio Society, 1960), pp. 34–5.

CHAPTER ONE

1. Colón, *Life*, p. 59.

CHAPTER TWO

1. Christopher Columbus, *Journal of the First Voyage* (Aris & Phillips, 1990), pp. 15–17.
2. Columbus, *Journal*, p. 9.
3. Columbus, *Journal*, p. 27.
4. Columbus, *Journal*, pp. 27–9.

CHAPTER THREE

1. Columbus, *Journal*, p. 29.
2. Samuel Morison, *Journals and Other Documents on the Life and Voyages of Christopher Columbus* (Heritage Press, 1963), p. 182.
3. Columbus, *Journal*, p. 29.
4. Columbus, *Journal*, p. 31.
5. Columbus, *Journal*, p. 33.
6. Columbus, *Journal*, p. 55.
7. J.M. Cohen, *The Four Voyages of Christopher Columbus* (The Cresset Library, 1988), p. 117.
8. Columbus, *Journal*, p. 121.
9. Columbus, *Journal*, p. 193.
10. Columbus, *Journal*, p. 167.
11. Columbus, *Journal*, p. 223.

Notes

CHAPTER FOUR

1. Cohen, *Voyages*, p. 136.
2. Cohen, *Voyages*, pp. 156–7.
3. Colón, *Life*, p. 149.

CHAPTER FIVE

1. Morison, *Journals*, pp. 263–4.
2. Morison, *Journals*, p. 279.
3. Morison, *Journals*, p. 287.
4. Morison, *Journals*, p. 286.
5. Colón, *Life*, p. 216.
6. Colón, *Life*, p. 219.
7. Morison, *Journals*, pp. 309–11.

CHAPTER SIX

1. Cohen, *Voyages*, pp. 286–7.
2. Cohen, *Voyages*, p. 293.

CHAPTER EIGHT

1. Felipe Fernández-Armesto, *Columbus* (Oxford University Press, 1991), p. vii.
2. Morison, *Journals*, p. 227.

BIBLIOGRAPHY

Bushman, Claudia L. *America Discovers Columbus: How an Italian Explorer Became an American Hero*, Hanover & London, University Press of New England, 1992

Cohen, J.M. *The Four Voyages of Columbus; Being his Own Log-Book, Letters and Dispatches with Connecting Narrative Drawn from the Life of the Admiral by his Son Hernando Colon and Other Contemporary Historians,* London, The Cresset Library, 1988

Colón, Fernando. *The Life of the Admiral Christopher Columbus*, tr. B. Keen, London, Folio Society, 1960

Columbus, Christopher. *Journal of the First Voyage*, ed. and tr. B.W. Ife, Warminster, Aris & Phillips, 1990

Dor-Ner, Zvi. *Columbus and the Age of Discovery*, London, HarperCollins, 1991

Dyson, John. *Columbus: for Gold, God and Glory*,

London & Toronto, Hodder & Stoughton/
Madison Press, 1991

Fernández-Armesto, Felipe. *Columbus*, Oxford &
New York, Oxford University Press, 1991

Granzotto, G. *Christopher Columbus: the Dream and the
Obsession. A Biography*, tr. S. Sartarelli, London,
Grafton Books, 1988

Hume, Robert. *Christopher Columbus and the European
Discovery of America*, Leominster, Fowler Wright
Books, 1992

Morison, S.E. *Admiral of the Ocean Sea. A Life of
Christopher Columbus,* 2 vols, Boston, Little,
Brown & Co., 1942

——. *Journals and Other Documents on the Life and
Voyages of Christopher Columbus*, New York,
Heritage Press, 1963

Phillips, William D. and Phillips, Carla R. *The Worlds
of Christopher Columbus*, Cambridge, Cambridge
University Press, 1992

Sale, Kirkpatrick. *The Conquest of Paradise: Christopher
Columbus and the Colombian Legacy*, London,
Papermac, 1992

Stannard, David E. *American Holocaust. Columbus and
the Conquest of the New World*, Oxford & New
York, Oxford University Press, 1992

Bibliography

Wilford, John N. *The Mysterious History of Columbus: an Exploration of the Man, the Myth, the Legacy*, New York, Alfred A. Knopf, 1992

POCKET BIOGRAPHIES

POCKET BIOGRAPHIES

POCKET BIOGRAPHIES

W.G. Grace
Donald Trelford

The Brontës
Kathryn White

Lawrence of Arabia
Jeremy Wilson

Christopher Columbus
Peter Rivière

Martin Luther King
Harry Harmer

For a copy of our complete list or details of other Sutton titles, please contact Emma Leitch at Sutton Publishing Limited, Phoenix Mill, Thrupp, Stroud, Gloucestershire, GL5 2BU